Poems

Daniel Lusk

Poems

Daniel Lusk

Maple Tree Editions
An Imprint of Onion River Press
191 Bank Street
Burlington Vermont 05401

Kin
Poems by Daniel Lusk
Copyright 2013 by Daniel Lusk
All rights reserved. No part of this book may be used or reproduced in any manner whatsoever without written permission except in the case of brief quotations embodied in critical articles and reviews.

Cover and book design by Laurie Thomas
Back cover photograph of author by Angela Patten
ISBN: 978-1-949066-05-0

Published by Maple Tree Editions, an Imprint of Onion River Press
191 Bank Street, Burlington, Vermont, USA

(Originally published by Wind Ridge Books in 2013, ISBN: 9781935922278)

for Angela

Contents

Preface ix
Acknowledgments xi

CHAPTER ONE
    Bull on the Roof 3
    Sermon of the Wolf 5
    Easter 6
    Meditation 8
    Uncle Charlie and Mole 9
    April 11
    Seasonal with Goats 13
    Beaver 14
    How Many Times 16
    Cures in Mud Season 17
    Sabbath Fool 18
    Boat, Pond, Girl 20
    Cardinal in the Blue Hour 22
    Now Playing at Carraig Binn 24

CHAPTER TWO
    To the Boy Saved from Drowning 27
    Rain 29
    The Long Mind 31
    Not the Coat 32
    Asking the Checkout Girl to Dance 34
    Toad 36
    Red Efts 37
    What Bird 38
    Charms 40
    Sweet Rock Amen 42
    Caveat 43
    In Which a Casual Lunch Prompts Profound Considerations and Noah the
    Navigator Reappears 44
    Still, Still, Still 46
    Bird with a Red Hat 47

Chapter Three

- Season of Cries 51
- Farewell 53
- Rumpelstiltskin 55
- If Not Holy 56
- Requiem for a Stranger 58
- Nocturne 59
- To Keep from Falling 60
- Red Ears and the Oak Woman 62
- Precision: A Poem of Thanksgiving 63
- Small Fires 65
- Meteor Moon 66
- A Room in the Woods 67
- Walk There 69

Chapter Four

- Ever Since Wednesday 73
- The Bear's Carol 75
- Near as I Recall 76
- Solstice Air for Machete and Bow 78
- Bark Beetle Tracks 80
- Last Solstice of a Thousand Years 81
- Christmas: Prayers and Songs 83
- Green Gospel 84
- Fugue 85
- Barred Owl 87
- New Year's Poem 88
- Meditation 89
- Woodchuck in Winter 90
- Great Horned Owl 91
- Bones and Bonafides 92
- Twelfth Night 94
- A Boiling Kettle, a Pelvis Bone 95
- Turkey 97
- Fisher 98
- The Bell Bird 99
- Uncertain Light 101

Preface

For more than a dozen years, Angela and I lived in a log house on a western slope of the Green Mountains in north central Vermont. The place we called *carraig binn* (Irish for "sweet rock") provided both the joys of encounters with wildlife and the challenges of husbanding a woodland acreage through the seasons. The poems in this collection celebrate the continuing presence in our local wilds of animals, birds and other creatures with whom we shared our lives.

The catalogue of visitors to our clearing included moose, bobcats, porcupines, courting foxes, weasels, woodchucks, raccoons, and deer. Rumors of catamounts persist among old-timers. Owls barked at evening, and sometimes woke us, hunting snowshoe hares in the night. Reading by the fire on those winter mornings I did not need to plow snow or sand the lane, I watched wild turkeys that came for the corn we had scattered.

Each spring a black bear showed off her rollicking cubs. In summer, flycatchers, hummingbirds, and dragonflies enlivened the air. Grouse drummed year-round from the margins. Warblers, wrens, grosbeaks, waxwings, Yellow-bellied Sapsuckers and Pileated Woodpeckers, Northern Flickers, Ovenbirds, orioles and finches brightened our lives with their calls and songs. Herons, Wood Ducks and mink fished the frog pond. Yellow-spotted salamanders lurked in their burrows. A snapping turtle laid her eggs among the foxglove. Hermit and Wood Thrushes fluted duets from the cliff top as we idled on our deck at day's end.

Rooted in such revelations, coupled with unbridled literary borrowings and my own inventions, these poems are offered with respect for my human family and for the many naturalists, gardeners, farmers, foresters and neighbors who helped us learn to live and work in rural Vermont.

—*Daniel Lusk 2013*

Acknowledgments

Thanks to editors of the following publications in which the poems in this collection first appeared:

Appalachia "Fisher"

The Beloit Poetry Journal "Woodchuck in Winter"

The Café Review "Twelfth Night"

The Chariton Review "The Bear's Carol," "Great Horned Owl"

Comstock Review "Small Fires"

GSU Review "To Keep from Falling"

The Iowa Review "Uncertain Light"

The Louisville Review "To the Boy Saved from Drowning"

The Midwest Quarterly "Meditation"

New Letters "Bull on the Roof," "Asking the Checkout Girl to Dance"

Nimrod International Journal "A Room in the Woods," "Nocturne"

North American Review "Sabbath Fool"

Oberon "Red Ears & the Oak Woman," "Rumpelstiltskin"

Seven Days "Rain," "Turkey"

The Southern Review "If Not Holy"

Spillway "Fugue"

Birchsong, anthology (Blueline Press, 2012) "Bull on the Roof," "Uncle Charlie and Mole"

The Breath of Parted Lips II, anthology (CavanKerry Press, 2004), "To the Boy Saved from Drowning"

"Making Our Own Light (Bucks County Poet Laureate Program, 2012) anthology, "Rumpelstiltskin"

I am also grateful to the Vermont Arts Council and the Vermont Arts Endowment for grants that supported the writing of many of these poems.

What will it mean to my grandchildren

that I fell north or west, that I sang this or that,

if they do not know what it meant

that silence became my religion?

ONE

Bull on the Roof

These frogs saved the world.
These frogs, fornicating in the lonely pond,
and these others singing all night in the trees.
They saved the world for silence.

All summer the rock cliff rises
behind the woods in secret,
looming behind birches and oak saplings,
their murmuring shadows suggesting voices
of soft-furred women in trees,
their elegant tails draping the branches.

These are images from a dream
I want not to wake from,
a dream where all the women's breasts freshen,
and I am the only child.

High overhead, bursts of east light
between stiff trunks thrust up
from roots anchored in rock, penetrating
the hidden places. As if winter
lived in a small house there,
next door to wind that blows only at night.

Among these wet caves there is nothing
I am afraid of. Not the yellow-spotted
salamander in the mud. Not the mud.
Not the libidinous jack-in-the-pulpit.

— continued

I fold my clothes, unfold my body
on a sundrenched rock
and listen to the hairy woodpecker at work.

One day when earth is exhausted
with pushing up and weary of swallowing.
When grouse tire of drumming.
When the brown-headed cowbird
has flown off with his bell
and the nests are empty.

When you and I
are like animals of the forest,
sated with heat.
When leaves give way to the rain
and weight of the sky.

We will go indoors to wait for the snow.
Winter will descend from its house.
The cliff will move closer
with icy teeth, huge in its power.

We will turn our backs and sit close to the fire.
We will hear the bull on the roof.
We will dream bright meadows and running water.

Sermon of the Wolf

Where is the woman
who can live one year as a human
and the next as a bird?

Where is the woman today
who has suckled a bear?

In old Ireland Fergne the physician
could tell from a man's face
what the illness was.
Just as he could tell from the smoke
that came from a house
how many were sick inside.

Boys and girls, we thought
we were the wolves' children.
That licking each other's faces
was food for our desires.
No one warned us not to go
into the fields of corn.
The corn would keep our secrets.

Who will tell us to be quiet
among the ignorant?
To cover our heads lest
we faint from truth.

Should we not ask such things?
We know that night is 11,400 miles wide.

Without bears or bats or fire,
what is there to worship?

Easter

Think of this rock
when snow has melted.
The bull ascends to the house
where the black bear slept all winter.

It's an old bull now
but still dangerous.

Imagine fog this morning.
Earth breathing, trees remembering
an old, wild road
close enough to a first principle.

How do I know this red eft
swept into light by my bamboo rake
is not the red woman
who attends the god.

Wet leaves roll away from a narrow hole
at the base of this moss-grown stone;
steam issues forth
the salamander stirs in her cave.

I remember Jenifer who heard
moss people singing
when she was naked under the stars
I believed her.

Hauling wet leaves in my arms
I do not look for truth
but for these raw appearances
truth is made of.

Frogs emerge from their beds
still brown and try their voices.
They sing light into the sky.

My mother's Easter card says
at the end, "we are failing fast."
Now what will rise?

Meditation

This is a holy place.
Mud people
keep the wind in pots.

It is the porcupine
in his quill robe,
the moose in his crown,
who made it holy.

See the star tracks
where the grouse walked,
unhurried, in the snow.

See the moss on the path
we swept free of leaves
and branches,
the moss covered stone.

Rain falls,
the pail and bowl
are filled with water.

We might have used it
to water the seedlings,
or for bathing ourselves.

Uncle Charlie and Mole

My great-uncle Charles was blind.
Sat next to Grandma's spinet-legged radio:
thin music, tinny war correspondent voices
turned up loud. Faced the window south,
rocking chair back to the coal stove
where I sat on the bustle stool to daydream
when I was bored with my book.

The story the cock grouse told
to the hen grouse was about the giant
and the king's three best teeth
and the cake, the crutch and the cure.

Today my story has a dead mole.

I don't know how he came to be
on winter's tired battlefield.

That's how it looked—the matted
grass, leaf litter, maze of trenches
where small digging beasts waged war
on cold and hunger in our yard,
out of sight beneath the snow.

I admired how Uncle Charlie worked
those butterflies of leather from the bag
beside his chair into piecework belts
with his stubby hands. How his spatulated fingers
plied the wooden crochet hook, deftly
knotting shreds of dresses into oval rugs.

— continued

These aimless tunnels in our yard
show no such purpose.
Mole dug his way, bare-flippered,
like a little walrus, delicate pink hind feet
kicked out a wake of severed grassroots,
worm feces, moss breath.
Swam efficiently in dirt.

I compare the mole to Uncle Charles,
whose prayers were smoke rings
I believe he never saw. A man
quite likely of another species
than those of us around him.
Whose condition had no cure.

For my own prayers to be answered,
bombs would have to fall the way
spring snow is falling, unexploded, melting
as they fall, becoming joyful torrents
in a roadside stream.

Missiles and other fire
from shoulder-mounted guns
would strike like seeds and pollen,
wintergreen and broom and helicopter
dragonflies would rise among these rocks and ridges
where the cock and hen grouse eat and drum.

Soldiers, citizens would all go home
to ordinary nightmares and love affairs,
to ordinary deaths.

April

Snow shower this morning.

We live at the border
between rain and snow,
winter and spring

where dogs become coyotes
and cats become wild

there are birds whose song can heal

mothers shed their clothes
and wander off,
naked as the girls they once were,
into the woods.

there are birds whose song can heal

We throw our hats into the air
at finding something
we thought we had none of.

We admit to nothing
and to everything.

there are birds whose song can heal

Lights in the sky
we worshipped only days ago
become myth

— *continued*

light from the great bull's horns.

It's not like the grouse drumming;
it's like when the drumming stops
and nobody owns
the fallen constellation
of their footprints in the snow.

there are birds whose song can heal

Absent the midnight caterwaul
of big cats or the girl
I mistook for them trying
with anything at hand
to make love to herself
like in the magazines

what else woke me:

cramps in my calves
from shoveling snow after
it melted down to heavy slush

there are birds whose song can heal

Seasonal with Goats

The bull again.
In spring, wood women
set out flowers—trillium,
anemones—to lure him
up the rock again.
Where he passes,
jacks-in-the-pulpit grow.

Snow melt, and we grow closer
to the rind of the world.

Remember now
the Brothers Gruff.
I loved that Troll.
He lived just under
all my fears. I heard him
coughing in the dark
so familiar
he should have had a name.

I'm looking for the big beast
when the little beast comes.

Some still believe a crust
of bread might be holy.
Let this sacred porridge represent
the promise in the world
for the return of equilibrium.

What could the women
want more than a little salt
and sweet water
at the close of a bitter season.

Beaver

Once upon a time there were no flowers.
Beauty did not yet exist.
Michael Pollan, *The Botany of Desire*

Who made the world?
Beaver did.

First light. First dog bark.
First runner on the road.

Night creatures—ermine, owl
and porcupine—recede
to shadowed quietude, maybe sleep.

Forest beat, the nightly daily *now*
the pulse of wind and hair and breathing,
with what some wish to find
as meaning in between.

There is no in-between.

Once this was only flow.
Leaves and ice clotted the streams
in season. White blossoms
like faery lights dotted the watercress,
and wisps of spray ghosted their sheen.

Then beaver came.
We lived because since then
there have been interruptions, blood,
much back and forth.

Sky shows its writing,
what it loves: geese crying over water
each bird glittering,
a broken strand of rhinestones.

Turkey hens ascend a slope,
an uncertain caravan of commas.

Moose tracks lead into the pond.
Here is a hollow log, marrow
bone enough for slumber.

How Many Times

How many times have I heard
the mud god say,
they died
when they died
they swallowed their words
and the mud
swallowed their meaning.

I dreamed of being forced
to separate from a dark child
and her mother
and awoke weeping.

It is known the spirit
of the dead remains three days
healing in its wrappings
then emerges
ascends like a butterfly
from a cocoon.

Daffodils begin to bloom
and I rake out the beds
careful of salamander women
in their caves.

Bare asparagus roots
I planted last year
have sprung up from the ground.

Cures in Mud Season

Let me cover your body
with my body.
Let us be lichen and water
and heated stones.

Let these incantations
draw fairies and saints
with their cures for fevers
their holy names.

To be sure there is power
enough to move heaven
and even wet earth.

We believe in credit cards
and microchips
as our people once believed
in goats' bladders and mother's milk.

The walls of the house
are weeping for ice and snow
melts on the roof.

They will pray over us
night and morning as over the crops
not yet planted:
may you be frightened neither
by lightning nor by passersby.

Whether morning be
an ill white thing
or an ill black thing,
and whether we be in it together,
let morning come.

Sabbath Fool

We have men loosening the nails on Noah's ark.
—Robert Bly

Two more sabbaths in a ditch
and what a small thing I am,
sore-shouldered,
plying my garden rake, my hoe.

An entire season of leaf-glut,
coupled with snow melt
off my mountain and lashing rain.
My lane running toward the sea,
washed into the town road.

Is the mud god happy?
Is the Brown-headed Cowbird pleased?
Are they jealous of this little path
up the hill, through the trees?

I will devote one day a year
to this ditch. Twenty years,
twenty days of diligence.
Of dig and carry from the stones
and root slime, taking wet leaves
in my blue wheelbarrow
to the swale in the trees.

Do I make much of a small thing?
This is not a death struggle
with forces of nature.
I am not Jacob and there is no angel.

These wet leaves, this mud
are not metaphors.
This red newt is not a symbol
of anything I am afraid of.

There is a dump truck perfectly
preserved in concrete
under the nuclear reactor
as evidence of ingenuity
and logic to a generation
picking through remains of a city.

When my beard is white
and I have been alone on the mountain,
walking a road so seldom traveled
a bird has anchored its nest to the grass
between the tracks,
I will mutter to strangers
the oldest obscenity I know.

I will not tell the name of the bird,
or where the deer lay,
or where to find sweet berries of wintergreen.
I will tell them The Terrible One
has given birth to the Terrible One.

Boat, Pond, Girl

This boat beside the pond is not seaworthy.
This pond is not a worthy sea
for going off in boats or deep imagining.
It keeps the little fish, green frogs,
and yellow-spotted salamanders
in mud tunnels underneath the boat.

The carnivorous, two-oared bug
without a name who eats the pollywogs.
Rain runs in.
A blue Buddha watches over.

Here is a moss bank with a copse of trees,
and a moss covered path
leading away through woods
toward habitations of grouse and hare.

If this is the "world navel,"
how shall we think of this old satellite dish
aimed at the ridge of mountains to the west
and no longer connected to anything.
I will think of it as the chakra of this place
and one day glimpse eternity.

Imagine the goldfish, debonair,
rising with their gold-headed canes
and strolling out among the trees,
singing a tune you can almost
remember hearing before.

I have a stick with a knob on the end.
Naked, I have stones in my pocket.

If I tap my stick on the ground,
is there a bush god who will answer
or a green girl to wave from the boat?

Cardinal in the Blue Hour

1
A hard rain, eating
the remaining ice and snow.

After the basement flood
the cat lifts her nose,
reading the wind.

Bread for the birds,
cracked corn, seed,
apple pulp for the deer

as snow melts
to the last amen.

2
As the last of the snow melts,
drops of blood
spring out of the ground

clumps of spurge, lovage,
lobelia, Stinking Benjamin

a raccoon handprint
fixed in mud.

The rewards of raking appear
because our heads are bowed.

These holes by the pond,
these smallest of caves—
dwellings of the meek.

3
After the blizzard of '46
the flood's detritus littered
the field around our bungalow

father in kitchen glare
threatened his throat
with the point of a paring knife

flash of blade
in the black eyes of the window
and night surrounding the house
like an unruly mob;
all of us in ragged unison crying.

4
First at the tips of a maple
by the frog pond.

Then, from ash
to hornbeam to poplar to birch
and away out of sight,

a single crimson strand,
a filament,
a thread
barely perceptible
as the blue vein on a newly pregnant
woman's breast.

Now Playing at Carraig Binn

A brand-new horn cannot account
for the sudden brilliance of trills
that May afternoon spring opens
its arms, and the kid across the way
emerges to practice his trumpet outdoors.

He's tuning his embouchure
over the swamp. Soprano sax
of termagant geese honking
their teen-aged goslings to flight.

Who knows if the cow moose refrains
from yelling because her mouth
dangles marsh marigold blossoms.

I'm hanging ripe store-bought grapes
from the deck to entice the Northern Oriole
high in a red oak on the bluff,
blowing a melodious cover
of yellow-bellied sapsucker's
snare drum licks on the shed roof tin.

Meantime, it's clear that a frog by our pond
unearthed a new riff
during the winter sabbatical.
The old shape notes plus a devilish trill.

At thirteen I solved in my dreams
the baffling *plie* of the swimmer's sidestroke,
the hurdler's cockeyed *grand jete*.

Having lost a front tooth
doing something less tricky,
today I'm relearning to whistle.

TWO

To the Boy Saved from Drowning

So in the days
the moss had no stones
wild turkeys picked among
ruins of winter
deer browsed the brown margins

there was only the smoke
of my fire and the Milky Way.

From nothing,
from empty slumber
great blue the preacher
knee deep in water,
tall in his tattered coat.

As it happened, I sunned
my young body on the wing dam
where the river swallowed a boy
whole and helpless as I was
at my own baptism.

I thrust my arm
into the rush of waters
and hauled him up,
dripping like a newborn
onto the thigh of the dam.

Three wives and at least
as many children, counting you.
Three bags of truth, I said.

— continued

And he rubbed his eyes,
glared at me as if I had
either pushed or fathered him.

You are the mud god himself,
he said. Now you know the truth.

Be silent, I replied. No talking.
The larger and small are singing.
The things will take it from here.

And we both
crawled off toward that
for which we had been saved.

Rain

On a day rain softens
until there is no air only water
I take off my clothes
and go naked into the garden
a water man among water trees
water shrubs water flowers

the green frogs too are water
jays and doves are water goldfinches
flash like light reflecting in water
the houses of chipmunks and snakes
by the pond are water

in a world of water
fish swim on the underside of water
only the woodchuck under the shed
a bureaucrat snuffling over papers
a poet with black eyes is dry

after drought even the fish dance
when we kiss when you take me
into your mouth when I take you
into mine the bee is inside the rose
the rose entirely humming

the child emerges headlong
from the humming waters of the mother
from her viscous parting
heart gills shut forever wet mouth opens
takes the mother in omphalos rush
still ringing in his ear canals the sound of rain

— continued

sister to a thrush's song at evening
over and over repeating inside and out
whip of the hummingbird's tongue
at courting apogee of pendulum
turtle's cracked mud eyes wet again
I cannot tell on which side
of water skin between us I am.

The Long Mind

I have seen at nightfall
blinking across the way
and thought I saw
a ship of burning lamps.

Opening the woods
I spared young oaks
for in these saplings
is the long future and knowing.

I believe there may be children
here among these roots
who pass for the children of gods.

Once in the dark age
was a naked race.
I wonder, do they live on
in these streams?

These intricate, improbable
nests of the orioles,
those skeletons we find in rocks
of lost, improbable animals

may be evidence
of something unresolved
some once upon the world
when we were holy.

Not the Coat

"He will not know what to do with so much sky."
—Pablo Neruda

Not the coat, merely,
but the name.
Not the beard which any goat
may grow, but the whole poet's heart
yearning for all that passed
for wisdom
when the world was young.

This is the poet at 63.
A prophesy.

Every year
before my birthday comes,
a village will again erupt
spontaneously
here in the yard—toadstools
like eggs on stilts.
What more am I certain of?

If I am, one day, old.
If the shadow of the owl
falls on the mouse,
I will be sure
that death and sanctity are both
contagious.
I will sleep
facing my native land.

Not the preachers, who are
cocksure,
but the scientists are looking
at the bodies of fallen birds
for Death.

I say listen to their calls.
Death has been there always.

If we want to find their souls
when they are gone,
look in the ears of their children.

Asking the Checkout Girl to Dance

They are always blond,
and I am always young.

For thirty years a woman
with long hair sits in the open window
over St. Sebastian's churchyard gate
in Salzburg, holding an apple.
Even then it was enough
the apple was a sinful red
and that she smiled at me.

Mine is a deferential, cautious yearning.
Even when I'm paying for these apples
and surprise myself by asking
the checkout girl to model for my drawings,
even when I ask her not to be fifteen
and tell her I'll be back in a few years.

If I had no memories,
would I have no regrets?

I come home in the dark
from work and cross the road to pluck
the daily paper from the box.
I hear water running in the ditch
from melting snow.
Up on the bluff the tall windows
of the new house in the trees are lighted.

I imagine having been inside
and intimate with the woman living there
whom I have never met.
And I am filled with deep regret
as though it turned out badly,
something sad already in the past.

Last night I saw the stars above the road,
how they moved out in the distance
like a whole city of the lost with searchlights.
And I was coming home.

Toad

The shaman throws magic hair
into the fire. Now

the new barn has a roof—dark red.

Not dark red of brothel curtains
in the French Quarter (imagine
the French Quarter of Jonesville)

more the red of a harlot's underwear.

I like to think there is at least one
harlot in every village
to keep fantasy alive, to stir
the gene pool.

That the black toad
under the building scrap
has a jewel hidden in his head.

Red Efts

On hemlock mulch
adolescent newts are invisible
until they move.

A pair surprised me,
as I climbed the stone steps
to deadhead the daffodils
and bergenia

two highwaymen, bandit
brothers in zoot suits.

Amazed at their disguise,
those bad boys,
I prepared to empty my pockets.

But they simply murmured
in some indigenous tongue,
then vanished among
the peonies and digitalis.
Swagger that said they've got
more than swag in their purses.

Did I mistake their meaning?
Were they step-guardian monks
in walking meditation?
Single hair of their beards,
their venerable faces, tall hats
obscured by fog that follows rain?

Was their demand not money
but to reveal
my earthly intention?

What Bird

What bird is that, whose song rings
over and over out of trees near the pond?

It is the man who exiled himself,
believing his song would save him
from the rigors of the world.

As in an old hero story,
for a long time nothing comes.
He mourns the loss of radiance and laughter.
Forgetting how to give and receive pleasure,
his skin grows hard around him.

Now he can kill without anger.
The knife in his sheath is ready.
He can learn the roaring of the wilderness
and a new song.

One day a woman comes
on her way from village to village.
Watching her, he observes
how terrifying and wild,
and her companions with her.

She carries puppets, first woman and first man.
First man's member is moveable and large.
First woman says their child will be born
at the time of eclipse, will be in danger.

She and her puppets embrace him,
all three talking at once.
This cloud, this shower of gold,
this bull this swan

when they lie all together
first woman shows herself naked
first man bursts into flame.
They do not care
that he is old and mad.

He opens his mouth to shout
and the bell-song of the cowbird
rings in his throat.

He shall have one queen,
three consorts, eighty-one concubines.
There have already been enough wives.

Charms

"There are ancient crones in Lerwick now who live by selling wind."
—from *The Golden Bough*, James Frazer

1
Who will bring the rain?
What women will seize a passing priest
and fling him into the well?

The frog choir from the neighbor's pond
chu-gunks like a kazoo band,
like boys beating the one arm
over the bare hand in the armpit,
like girls beating their hands on water
or slapping their wet breasts together
to bring down rain.

The child of my child
is come of age and leaving home.
Surely pouring water
over her ripe body
could cause rain to fall.

2
I said to her:
"Strike the love-stone lightly.
You shall have love for a time.

3
Today a large porcupine appeared
in the yard. He drew himself up
to show us how he had blackened
his muzzle; as he lumbered off

we saw how he had tucked up
his skirt of quills like women do
who walk in circles to placate the sky

who piss on the fire so the black smoke
will darken clouds
and bring down rain.

4
He will go now and wash his face.
Has the mud god grown deaf?
Have the frogs abandoned us?
Do the very snails weep
for want of rain?

Sweet Rock Amen

How is it the woman
climbed into this tree
from the floodwaters swirling below
and gave birth to her child?

Sweet rock, amen.

Good god of the tree.
Good god of the helicopter
come down from the sky.
Good ordinary god, who replies
only to the question put to him.

Sweet rock, amen.

Hearing such news from the radio,
I stand in my kitchen,
watching a barred owl watching
a pan of fish
I left on the fieldstone wall.

Fierce god standing still in a tree,
blinking out from your mask of white bone.
Wind loves those feathers.
Whisper of death today
a rumor in the woods.

Sweet rock, amen.

The world is as large as my prayers.
The god is as small
and all my questions are trivial.
I am awestruck by ordinary things.

> *—for them: Sophia and daughter Rosita*

Caveat

The government can do nothing
about the dragonfly's incorrigible child,

or about elegant wood ducks
who arrive to eat the pale-bellied frogs
on their first day up from the mud,
or about these spring-loaded bullfrogs
eating leopard frogs,

or about the big cat patient
in the shadow of the ledge for mallards
to fall asleep on their nest of twigs

or about the striped chipmunks
playing hide-the-acorn
among the rocks

or about these women stepping naked
among shadows and dappled light.

The government can do nothing
about a fire in the breast
of the woman with a damp photo
of a son in her apron pocket

or the child in the center of the circle
whose voice is an assassin
all fall down

or the one outside the circle,
skipping and dancing,
a kerchief or a rose or a flag
trailing from her small hand,
when she becomes in a moment
a lover.

Let the government do
what it can do.

In Which a Casual Lunch Prompts Profound Considerations and Noah the Navigator Reappears

Never mind what Moses would have said
about rules or Nietzsche about wine
above all else it is images I love

the color of the dress she shrugs
from her cream-and-caramel shoulders,
the pallor of her face as he is tearing away
her clothes to try his best to save her

and of course this happens in costume dramas.
Think yourself how feelings are a weak
translation how the heart
is just as likely to feel one thing as another

my eyes leaking at a line from an immortal scene
because of irony like lantern light on their faces
while around me in the theatre people laugh.

A vixen runs dead ahead as if the edge
of the headlights were a magic fence
surely she doesn't feel the same way I do
about this sudden convergence of our lives

any more than the arts editor across the table
lifting her drink mid-sentence
past the soft indentation that is like a thumbprint
at her throat feels her heart begin
to pace among its rooms because of what I said.

Noah looks out across the endless water
and seeing the weather finally at ease
with not a stone or rug or barrel stave in sight,
for no apparent reason says to his son:
"Send the dove."

Still, Still, Still

A machine bird repeats its one note.
Gossamer snowfall, torn hem of winter.
Snowshoe hare tracks. Tree shadows.

In old time the planets were kept in boxes
by an old chief. Like the sacred pipe
White Buffalo Woman brought.

These days as Lame Deer said
anonymous old woman keeps it
wrapped in deerskin under her bed.

When the earth was made,
I was there.

This is not a boast.
It was yesterday.
Ask the rock,
when she awakes.

Tall man faced the crowd,
a Cooper's Hawk with one eye
on his gloved hand.

Then the barred owl with one wing.
This is how the wild world
will one day be.

Did I mention the cold.

Bird with a Red Hat

—after a painting by Vermeer

The gender of the adolescent
pileated woodpecker, knocking beaks
with its insolent reflection
in our patio door,

the name of the model gazing
from beneath scarlet feathers
of her bumptious hat,

the true identity of the artist
who painted her insouciant gaze—

these remain uncertain
after four days or four hundred years.

Bird lovers in Paris, Jonesville,
Amsterdam, we must be content

even as we content ourselves
to suffer the unbidden canter
of our hearts
as we recall a faded morning
we awoke inhaling the perfume
of someone only just arisen
from the pillow next to ours and gone
without the coat check of a name.

— continued

We learn to forego certainties,
to live as if the flaming crest
of a bird at our door, or bold feathers
on a hat—like sealing wax
on an envelope addressed to us
in a familiar hand—were signs
that signify but do not prove.

THREE

Season of Cries

*Then shall the sheep be adorned with flowers
and cattle driven from their stalls with song.*

Late summer and all
the fledglings—tufted tit,
rose-breasted grosbeak, chickadee
and jay—cry out in tuneless spasms,
shrugging their shoulders
of hand-me-down feathers,
imploring harried parents
to fill their beaks and gullets.

Their monotony shakes
the lilacs and bee balm, makes
the gardens nervous
day in and day out.

In old time I dressed in white
silk trousers and shirt, white linen shoes
and went out in disguise
to teach the young ones to sing.

They lay on their backs
by the ancient piano, and I pressed
my closed hand firmly against the swale
between their ribs and their bellies
and so
they surprised themselves
with their sounds.

— continued

The air,
like their heels and scapulas at rest,
quivering around them.

I think they have thanked me
again and again—long since the time
of our lessons has faded
and I am truly anonymous—
only husbands and lovers
to hear their wild true voices.

Farewell

I can hear them breathing.
High above the road
where hemlocks anchored
in the rock begin,
I hear them and look down
to see two cyclists
laboring.

They hear nothing
but their bodies' work.
I am speaking to a branch
and breathing quietly.
Above me in the trees
big cats and keening raptors
watch and know we are alive

and hear us breathing.

I have heard that a physician
may by accident swallow
the soul of a patient
and that death will follow.

A thousand miles away
mother is dying.
On the phone I hear
her breathing in the space
where she cannot complete
a simple utterance.

— continued

Her footprints in the sand
of a bygone road, when she
was running from the house
her slender back
and loping stride
the screen door rebounding
the flies confused

opening a space between us
I believe I never closed
completely
until I found myself
completing all her sentences

until now on a plane.

I've never seen a moose
except in pictures
but I know
what awkwardness is possible
and still cannot distinguish
love from heartache.

I climbed down the bluff
and stood with one arm fast
around a slender oak

and heard the low
breathing of the earth,
around staccato breathing
of the cyclists, knowing
high above me on the rock
the large ear of the mountain
listened

Rumpelstiltskin

In the time of original things—
thatch, broth, paving stones—a physician
might have enjoined her to dip her shirt
seven times in a south-running stream.

Yesterday, grandchildren murmured
in distant corners of the room.

Tonight she is out of options.

Now she is old, she wills
him to come back to her.
Envisions his mischievous smile
in the dark. Tries to conjure his bizarre
physique, the aura that had lingered.

Sleepless for the pain,
she is enveloped by the odor of silence.
Once more, she whispers
to the ashen light above her bed.

Wasn't it enough to know his name?

She hears the whine of wind in the eaves.
Almost familiar voices below stairs.
The whinjing of the raven's wing beats.
Thunder. Then rain.

If Not Holy

When we learned
that we were orphans now,
all the brothers gathered
and her tribe around us.

I myself left my window,
left the red newt in the shadow
of the raging zucchini blossom,
left the handprints of raccoons
and opossum on the sodden
maple leaves like dried blood
along the corridors of woods,
left the hair of wild cats, knitted
into nests of songbirds.

Not our mother but an effigy mother
in the vestibule.
We looked to faded photographs
to see her smiling, in her arms
those children we have been.

How we sang!
And if the old church cracked
with joy, our hearts were broken
and their fullness pouring out.

When the young men of us
had carried the white box to the field,
the blind preacher once again denied
the new name of the old
is always Dead.

Then were we asked to go away
and not to see the casket sink
for all we know into everlasting
solace of the earth.

What was it we believed?
What was she
who would agree at last to leave?

What else but love and loss
would call and cause
that intensity of song we did?
I say it was our home.

We sang our wild songs
and agreed to live on.
Her tribe and legacy.

So I returned to smell
of wood smoke in the silent house
like residue of vanished life.
To the gray heron
immersed to his chest
in the freshened lily pond.

To the feeling that
some glade, some moss green
stone in these woods could be,
if not holy, at least
a place to kneel down.

Requiem for a Stranger

Cedar waxwing lies on the deck
outside the counterfeit thoroughfare
of our patio doors

as if misled by voices of faeries
as if fallen asleep in her sage green
poet's coat, patent-black shoes.

As if, by dreaming, she might recall
where she mislaid her red bracelet,
her black Egypt mascara brush.

How many times a day do I blink,
so many times I am blind.

I will surround the house
with a pattern of zygodactyl tracks
to confuse the bad bird spirits.
Will call for robins to cover her body
with white peony petals and rue.

She has given up salt
to follow the traces of the blessed feet.

In this sanctuary,
hermit thrush will know to sing.

Nocturne

I heard one owl
before I went to sleep.
Was roused in the night
by another.

The first one sighed;
the second barked.
How lucky not to be
a mouse or hare.

I begin to share
the old man's confusion.
Sometimes I am his son;
sometimes he is mine.

He writes that he sits
crooning poems in his room,
death in one corner
and old age in the other.

Bad company, these two,
and the other ones
that pass in the hall,
who creep and trot and hoot.

Listen.
Who cooks for you?
A fine question for the old one.

There was
and there was not
a man.

To Keep from Falling

Long, long time
at the other end of the dream

we lived in trees
our tails hung down
so infants tired of clinging
to our fur could sleep below,
their fists closed tight.

We heard claw-footed ones
come to the pond to drink.
We eaves-dropped on tree gods
and chiming stars.

When the leaves exploded,
raining fire, we came down.
We began to learn.

We came to know wild women
of the nether wood
who could anoint their bodies
and be invisible.

Who threw their breasts
over their shoulders
when they ran.
And we ran after them.

No going back for fear.
Our mothers have become
somnambulists and have no tails.
Our winds blow from the north.

We rise at night
and look out our windows
to see what snow has fallen.
Enough to tell what is
from what is not.
Teeth from not teeth.

We sleep, clinging
to each other's fur.

Red Ears and the Oak Woman

Good autumn work,
splitting oak rounds for the winter fire.
Around me, colors nobody but clowns,
exotic dancers, maybe pontiffs wear.

My friend, Red Ears, sits
on the woodpile to advise.
He says oak has a g-spot
when it dries. I drive the heavy blade
over and over in a line
of futile nicks across the grain.

And then the lovely pock
when I discover he is right again.
One more true mighty stroke,
the oak round splits.

Look, says Red Ears, she let you win.
A fleshy worm clings
to the torn grain where it fell apart
as if she'd held it tight between her thighs
while I sweated, unaware.

Now the two halves pop
in two again, and easily again
as I persist until the open grain
reveals the dress she wore last season
as a stripe-winged, fragile creature
of another kind when she crawled in.

Orioles and scarlet tanagers
swim in the mirror of the pond.
Goldfish among the poplar
branches. I am enthralled.
Red Ears is gone.

Precision: A Poem of Thanksgiving

The Mars probe is lost,
a near miss the engineers have said.
They sit in silence, listen
to the pinging of the stars.

If I throw a rock
at the broken outhouse in a clearing
near the ancient sugar maples
on the ledge a quarter mile away,
the one thing certain is
that it will hit something
if only Earth.

Poet John Berryman threw himself
from a bridge at the Mississippi River
and hit the ground.
It was a practice throw
but he wouldn't get another.

I am much nearer the end of my life
than when I contemplated suicide
at twenty-five, but no more
certain or less prepared to be amazed.

Thirteen wild turkeys hurry
by the side of the road, and I wonder
if theirs is an initiation.
Remember the boys who looked up
when looking was forbidden
were killed and cooked and eaten.

— continued

This is the Creator god's body
on these pewter plates with paper doilies.
This is the blood in these tiny tumblers,
difficult for the old ones, with ringing
in their ears and arthritic fingers, to hold.

We were good and ate well,
and washed down our bread with wine.
There were others, watching,
eating their prayers.

Small Fires

At 400 degrees the wood stove
begins to speak. Mole
emerges from a snowbank
onto the tread-marked sea
of the lane. An honest error,

being born thus at solstice.
He was following his star, mining
his rootscape bare-handed as any potter,
unmolested by bell-ringing clergy,
heretics, judges or tradesmen.

Nobody knows about the man
who knocked at the door
of a modest house on a dead-end street,
frozen turkey in a paper sack.
About the man who opened,
faces of a woman and child pale
behind him in the dim light. Or
which of these I was.

Mole was keeping his secrets.
Keeping Castor behind him.
And now plunged into who knows
what blazing company
on the darkest day of the year.

Meteor Moon

Full moon tonight
the two of us trudging
up our lane through deep snow
moonlight drifting into footprints
we made early this morning,
carrying heavy truck tires
down to the road.

A meteor shower predicted
we put out the torchlight and see stars
still overhead. Light from a new neighbor's
windows, a dog barking.

In Ireland on the way to Cork
at dusk we passed a smithy,
spray of stars from the forge
showering out the door.

We climb this hushed territory home,
only thud of our feet
and ghostly tree shadows.
We long to see some fierce animal,
knowing we would be afraid.

Winter is animal enough.
Eyes of places among the rocks
are open, and the shy ones,
the furry dark ones with keen teeth
hunting among them.
No peace for nut eaters,
or the snowshoe hare not yet white,
frozen in our path.

A Room in the Woods

To sit on a stone
with my back to a tree.

I have a chair and a wall.

To look away to a hillside,
rising from a stream below.

A floor of wild oats
and false hellebore.

This is my room—the door
and windows wherever they need to be.

The odor of solitude
like peppermint, sprung
from a cribbage of holes
a woodpecker tapped in a birch.

My young friend H recalled
waking in a thatched hut
to see a man of the village
standing over her, watching her sleep.

J said on Reunion Island
the homes also have no doors,
and people meander like cousins
in and out of each others' houses.

— continued

Deep claw marks of a grizzly bear
etched the door of DB's cabin in Arlee.

"Intimacy," "privacy"—these
are meaningless without the word "door."

I draw pouch and pipe
from my pockets, a match
to spend a solemn hour.

I always imagined living alone
in the maid's room
of a brownstone on 63rd Street.

Now the cat is dead
and one less heart beating in the house.

I read somewhere
that rue was called "meadow rue"
to ease the regret.

Walk There

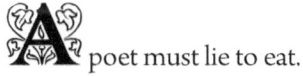poet must lie to eat.

If you would know him,
go to his house.
Do not listen to his speech
or his moaning.
Do not ask him to find objects
hidden in the rooms.

See how he walks around his house,
singing songs.
See where he has tapped his stick
and where he places his chair.

Look that way. Walk there.

FOUR

Ever Since Wednesday

—for Lufuno Tshikororo

Lufuno is dead in South Africa.
And I am sanding the driveway by snow light.
Tomorrow the star-like tracks of grouse
will lead across the porch and away into the woods.

I cannot see snow falling,
though the hillside is luminous. What I believe
to be snow touches my face, whispers
in the night around me. Whispers on all sides,
in branches of hemlocks and maples,
in rock shadows, on shimmering ground.

I believe when our loved ones
make themselves invisible by closing their mortal eyes,
they remain with us, immaterial.
Because we need them and because we fail
to understand what is insubstantial can still love us.

Where are the ten children
who folded their desires into waxed paper boats,
filled them with sand for ballast,
and pushed them onto the current of the river?
Boats to be prayers for the world.
Some, of course, begged instead for new bicycles.

Will the god who lives under the aqueduct,
diverting water for drivers to wash their buses
and bartenders to splash into drinks,
want payment for carrying our desires?

— continued

Now you are returned to your village,
is the god there happy?

Ten shovels full of sand take an hour to scatter,
down the hill and back, and I have no desire
but to finish the work, go inside, and close the door.

In the first decade of the Fifth Century
Barbarians crossed the frozen Rhine
and the Roman Empire it is reported fell quietly.

People walked their dogs, went to concerts, watched
the Home Shopping Network, drove their children
to soccer practice, talked of betrayals of public trust.

When were we chosen to walk upright
or ascend like sated hawks toward heaven?
I have fashioned a rule:
When the black bear stands, do not stand near him.

For the second time on this ice
I pick myself off my back,
humbled again by falling.

I listen awhile for the bark of a fox
or an owl's query, and I am not alone.
Off to the southwest a shooting star
marks the slate of the sky, then erases itself.

The Bear's Carol

Winter solstice.
Clink of glasses. Far-off songs.

We're warm here, where snow
ticks down on hemlocks, repeats
and repeats as if it were news
and we didn't believe it.

Having sung those fat months
to her brawling triplets
as she browsed witch hazel leaves,
foraging for butternuts and thimble berries,
grubbing larvae from the rotted stump
by our stony wall, now bear sleeps
in a secret crevice on the hill.

What was the bear's carol
about, then? About her own
hairy god, her own child born in a cave,
her descent into dark and the miracle.

South wind today sings
of magnolias, catfish, jambalaya.
Wild turkeys by the road
in bright spring attire,
old-fashioned girls with red ribbons
sewn into their brown petticoats.

Bear dreams a faint rumor
of light to come.

Near as I Recall

I saw dawn come, a fleet of boats
with tiny lights and snow
was falling and had fallen.
In my torchlight trees raised their hands.

"Present," sang the children
in our one-room school
as names were called.

The hutches where dry sand
is closeted glow tonight.
I leave the torchlight there,
to haul one shovelful at a time
to scatter along the lane.

A small light travels far
over the snow.
A little sound, the same.

The neighbor's dog hears me, thinks
I am Sasquatch. The neighbor
awakened on the bluff across the road
hopes I am. Or else the hairy man
who scuffles in her dream.

The lighted hutch becomes
the little schoolhouse
winter mornings we came early,
sniffling, feet and fingers numb,
to help Miss Phares
kindle the furnace fire
with old spelling papers.

Such long shadows now.
Sanding the lane by hand
when snow is on the way again
is like devotion to a woman
who is already planning her escape.

Solstice Air for Machete and Bow

—*for Ellie*

Call it winter. Say forgetfulness.

Snowdrifts curl around the woodshed,
the new barn. Wind worries
noiseless flames in the wood stove.
We hear nothing of trucks,
ghosting along the interstate.

We hear instead the crack and spit
of memory:
a tiny scar round her index finger,
a trace on the skin,
like a twig under snow.

Everywhere I go—in hotels, subways,
under bridges, at the foot of stairs,
I listen for her violin.

Orderly stands of lodge-pole pine
flourish on fire-swept
Montana mountainsides
where her machete spared them.

A naked girl in Red Wing boots
with her companion nanny goat.

If I go there now, I will
listen for the measured pizzicato
of her knife. The glissando of goat's milk
spreweled into a pitcher cooling
in a hidden spring. At dusk

for strains of Brahms and Schumann
and an owl's antiphonal refrain.

I come closer every day to finding her again.

Bark Beetle Tracks

As we learned to read,
those strange, tidy marks on the page
bore little evidence of the cat's
stiff whiskers, or the smell the dog
left steaming by the road.

No hint of the fire off
mother's comb and hair,
or the smoke of father's breath.

Cold fingers of baptistry water
clutched our genitals
and drowned our eyes,
masking the big idea that love
was everywhere and baffling and good.

By the time we could scrawl
clumsy messages, heirs
to Plato, Moses, Seneca, we tried
to guess how puffs of smoke
a friend could see across the county
might announce "deer plenty"
or "come quick."

Inside snug bark of paper birch
exploded by the splitting maul
are weird, truncated phrases,
wild, existential messages,
the signal, smut and poetry of a species.

Last Solstice of a Thousand Years

I believe there is
no ice god.
No heart, no mercy.

Hiking up the ledge,
pulling myself by cold arms
of striped-maple saplings.
My hands like pitchforks.

If there is a god of ice, tonight
he is disguised.
What does it mean, he is
wearing his brother's coat?

No voice but wind,
which eats sounds of small birds
speaking from the winter trees.
What it says tonight may be untrue.

Snow falling, and a train
calls
far below by the river.

For a time I follow tracks
of a large cat. When I lose them,
I move away from the trees

— continued

and think of everyone I ever knew
who died—father, grandfather,
grandmother, the aunts and uncles,
lovers dead and gone,
a few grand ideas.

And they appeared
in that blue hour, quickened.
On earth I am happy.
Overhead there are flies on the moon.

Christmas: Prayers and Songs

Birdsong in the fire,
as burning wood gives up its ghosts.
I think I hear a distracted, random tune
once whistled by a traveler, passing by.

This morning the pond is burning,
goldfish and salamanders and frogs
silver and gold.
And snow continues falling.

Who comes up the mountain?
What god, materialized with antlers glowing?

The large god who made the world
and wandered through it as a beggar—even
the king's servant leading the kitchen burro
spits on him. Will he huddle by this fire?

Will this day be the question
and an answer to his prayers?

Green Gospel

Lugging the last split firewood
to the house, I disturb
the mouse's nest again, this time
in shredded birch bark.

After a long, deep winter
ruffed grouse, whose drum
I believed to be the heartbeat
of the mountain, is gone.

Woodpecker on the suet bag
teaches her young galoot
to freeload for himself.

Once we were glad for bowls
of broken bread in milk
to quiet our howling bellies.

Magi come back every year
for that same star,
and every year a child is born
to the one village virgin.

Try not to mistake "perennial"
for "eternal." Do not confuse
wind with ancient voices.

Fugue

Any old shepherd
might have a better life than me.
Might sense,
in the swirl of moonrise over the shed roof,
of fog moving among those creek-bed trees,
or stranger's shadow on the path,
some evidence
the seam of Nature is revealed.

Here I am,
the morning light,
the tangle of trees,
wild beasts inside me.

Divine songs,
the fearsome beat of horses galloping round
the foot of the wooly-headed, hoar-frosted mountain.
Flower of in-breath,
jets of mist shooting out of the ground.

A virgin taken by surprise
just there by those rocks
where the dog is buried.
Air, pregnant with wing beats.
A word, spoken by a tree.

Solstice–damn! Cold enough to hear star music.

— continued

What wildness do I have
except this ache close to my heart.
The old thud music, the old visceral wish.

Far from the house,
far from the road,
emptiness
and the prattle of human voices.

Dawn light comes, glacial, bearing a prison ship
with fifty women at the oars.
What might I achieve in this day?
In such a day as this?

Barred Owl

Hunched in his morning coat
over a shot of Lemon Heart rum,
he watches the tattoo of a butterfly
emerge from the cocoon
of the bartender's shirt each time
she bends to the ice bin.

He recalls a young barfly,
summer dress loose and revealing
most of her skin, moved
to the barstool next to him,
put her tongue into his ear.

Little did she suspect,
her loveliness coyly tendered,
and his predacious desire aroused,
where that ear had been.

Years later, sitting alone on a branch,
your pants too short,
watching a plate of leftover salmon
on the fieldstone wall,

wouldn't you bark now and then
into the frozen air?

New Year's Poem

Just when we think this
new year is going to be a repeat
of all the others, bits of things
we already know happening

as we knew they would—same
white sales, same nieces' weddings,
same wrecks, same sermons,
same quavery sopranos in the choir,
same fireworks over the same lake—

all at once, thank you James
     here comes everybody!

Five wild turkey hens plummet
from the sky with flouncing
of skirts and flurry of feather boas
and in random order.

Yesterday they had come single file,
over snow-buried stile and stones,
one trident foot in front
of the other like the remnant
of a regiment returning from war.

Today they flew in, cascading
through the trees heavy
and ungainly, matronly
as cannon balls or WWII B-29s

and went to work raking
the snow by the pond for cracked corn
I put out, their standard issue dewlap neckties
twitching with practiced abandon.

Meditation

Where the pond will rise
as deep snow ebbs
slow-wise,
brilliant light casts oak
and hemlock shadows.

I could read some scripture,
find my keys,
or earn a tracking merit badge
by this religious light.

My gaze is lifted
to the diadem of rock that crowns
the cliff, to head and horns,
to granite cradle
of this dazzling, late winter moon.

Bear sleeps, woodchuck no doubt,
and yellow birches their benign slumber.
I keep winter watch with ermine,
coyote, fisher, owl—stealthy,
swift, sharp-eyed, rapacious.

Woodchuck in Winter

Orpheus stirs in the dark
to the blinking of the digital clock.
Power out, time stopped,
it's no use turning on a light.
House buried comfortably in snow.

He won't bother to put batteries
in the radio for news.
Thoreau was right: theft happens, fires,
murder. When they repeat, it's only gossip.

He recalls the scents of green grass,
pungent broccoli, sweet basil.
He favors parsley, good for the prostate.
When spring comes he'll remember
what it's for as the young
bare their tattoos again. For now

these invisible walls may as well
have trees flowering with butterflies.
And glyphs of soft-furred females
he's encountered—love and loss
his only ailments. As for a theology,
the same as for politics: there is fat
for now and fat for later.

That humans have souls is a nice conceit.
That they preserve their carcasses, quaint.
Death is not a mystery to disturb one's sleep.
He contents himself that the deity,
as someone once remarked,
"isn't on a cloud; she is the cloud."

Great Horned Owl

To sleep in a room
in the old city wall is not
a great cure for wandering.

Neither is the sight of owl wings,
fringed like antique lamps,
silent shade, swaying among the trees.

Leaning on a pine trunk,
head on backward, squinting in snow light.
Caught out after all the bars
have shut and no breakfast for the kids,
she can't go home.

She's been reading Augustine, Aquinas,
Calvin—those great butchers
of the human heart. Images of tortuous
hereafters disturb her sleep.

Now it's a new year and terrible rumors
have been published. She wears a dark
reputation. When she takes to the air again,
it will matter little whether "all rise"
before her awful, imperious shadow

or, like children in a circle
pretending to be stricken,
"all fall down."

Bones and Bonafides

January 6, some call Epiphany.
When all the ornaments and lights,
the clip-on birds and bows and stars,
the horned and humped *papier mache*
exotics were packed away again
in wrinkled tissue and old yuletide wraps,

I took the naked tree outside
and stuck it in the snow.

Next morning I could see
how makeup artists overnight
had powdered it to look
like any living fir, the way the actress
Helen Hunt becomes a waitress
at the Blue Line Diner
or mother of three in a highway toll booth
or your secret love
behind the library Reference desk.

Snow had been predicted;
now huge flakes were skidding
down like pieces off the morning's light.
Chickadees peat-peat and repeat.
Why were we so afraid
the sky would fall?

As I write this I am thinking
of my mother's face
as she pushed a biscuit
whole into her mouth, too weak
to bite or chew.

Back in her room I brushed
her hair, careful with the yellowed bruise.
She hated makeup, though
she wouldn't have minded
a little snow at Christmas.

Twelfth Night

Epiphany: a crystal hammer.

We dismantle our tree,
admire each treasured ornament,
wrap and pack them all away.

Forest choir at dawn,
the haunting F-sharp
of the wind-blown trees
along the gambrel of the bluff.

Prayer-flag leaves
of young beeches by the gray,
snow-hatted birdbath

their low, muttered eccles.

A single cardinal on the snow;
his medieval red relieves
the January monochrome.

Snowplow man inside
the cowl of his black truck
comes and goes in corridors of white

his yellow blade a cup, an ordinary mystery.

A Boiling Kettle, a Pelvis Bone

The man with fever does not want
baked brie and apples, nor his favorite wine,
nor even gourmet coffee with fresh cream.

He thinks not at all of sex.
The woman curled around him is welcome
for her naked heat; so is the cat
pressed tightly to his other thigh,
keeping out the draft.

He wants, more than anything,
more than applause, than love or money,
to have these chills subside,
for these sore bones to lie still together.
Something hot may sound appealing,
cornmeal mush or cream of wheat
with heated milk and maple syrup.

But he cannot move his bare hand
from beneath the quilts even to reach for water,
cannot raise himself except when driven
out into the cold room, headed for the toilet,
shuddering, sometimes not quite soon enough.

Once in Montreal between trains
at a subway stop he heard sweet music
of anonymous violin, for perhaps two
minutes, and was overcome.
He dreams of leading two blind men
through a strange city, searching
for a restaurant only they will recognize,
no telling how.

— continued

Awakened, sleep clothes damp with sweat,
bright moonlight casting shadows
on the snow draws him to the window.
A single deer beneath the birdfeeder,
eating corn discarded by the doves.

Krishna said: no one can live and not die.
Therefore, do not grieve.

Turkey

Wild tom yesterday at the far
edge of woods
cautiously measuring

snatching bugs from fronds
of cinnamon and interrupted ferns.

Today under the bird feeder
still alone among the dross
of sunflower seeds

I imagine him
the Judas of turkeys,
outcast and made brave
by his hunger

or the Magdalene of turkeys
shunned
for being most
what the others need.

Fisher

Streaks across the road ahead
into the winter trees,
a vivid, long-tailed shadow
against the frozen snow.

Confirmation that belief
is irrelevant. The world is,
and I am in it.

This fierce, shaggy weasel
does not mean anything, is not
either less or more

than the snowshoe hare,
than a puff of wind or a knife,

than the blood
on its hot gums.

The Bell Bird

Snow patches nearly gone,
Brown-headed Cowbird
is back with his comely mate
and the glass harp.

The floor of the woods
is alive with noise.

We wintered well.
There was bread
and wood for the fire
and fresh water.

Today, six geese in the field
and one in the flood.

We planted our garden:
one row each of onions,
lettuce and carrots;
two hills of cucumbers,
zucchini for the blossoms.

A hawk strutted in and out
of the clearing to jeering of jays.
Cowbird withdrew
and swallowed
and rang.

There is no sound
of grouse drumming.
My mother is still gone.

— continued

Back home, people
liked to say things like:
"six months to the day."

The world is green now
and promising.
This is the answered prayer.

Uncertain Light

Let me follow for now
the mind of the bear
in a forest of souls.

One who hears weeping.

Who may be attracted
by the uncertain light of my torch
where I lie in wet snow
under my truck to fasten
the tire chains, sleet
turned to rain on my face.

Who knows I am singing
under my breath.

www.ingramcontent.com/pod-product-compliance
Lightning Source LLC
Chambersburg PA
CBHW021443080526
44588CB00009B/668